Exploring Earth and Space

Space Probes

Lorraine Stiegler

NEW YORK

Published in 2013 by The Rosen Publishing Group, Inc.
29 East 21st Street, New York, NY 10010

Book Design: Katelyn Londino

Photo Credits: Cover Paul Fleet/Shutterstock.com; p. 4 Cristi Matei/Shutterstock.com; p. 5 Neo Edmund/Shutterstock.com; p. 6 Omikron Omikron/Photo Researchers/Getty Images; p. 7 commons.wikimedia.org/wiki/File:Mariner_2_in_space.jpg/Wikipedia.org; p. 8 Detlev van Ravenswaay/Picture Press/Getty Images; p. 9 commons.wikimedia.org/wiki File:CW0131775256F_Kuiper_Crater.png/Wikipedia.org; p. 10 commons.wikimedia.org/wiki/File:Mars_atmosphere.jpg/Wikipedia.org; p. 11 Jurgen Ziewe/Shutterstock.com; p. 12 commons.wikimedia.org/wiki/File:Saturn_during_Equinox.jpg/Wikipedia.org; p. 13 commons.wikimedia.org/wiki/File:Voyager.jpg/Wikipedia.org; p. 14 commons.wikimedia.org/wiki/File:Cassini_Saturn_Orbit_Insertion.jpg/Wikipedia.org; p. 15 Space Frontiers/Stringer/Archive Photos/Getty Images; p. 16 AFP/Stringer/AFP/Getty Images; p. 17 commons.wikimedia.org/wiki/File:Mars_Pathfinder_Lander_preparations.jpg/Wikipedia.org; p. 18 commons.wikimedia.org/wiki/File:Mars_pathfinder_panorama_ large.jpg/Wikipedia.org; p. 19 Science & Society Picture Library/Contributor/SSPL/Getty Images; p. 20 commons.wikimedia.org/wiki/File:NASA_Mars_Rover.jpg/Wikipedia.org; p. 21 commons.wikimedia.org/wiki/File:Juno_Mission_to_Jupiter_(2010_Artist%27s_Concept).jpg/Wikipedia.org.

Library of Congress Cataloging-in-Publication Data

Stiegler, Lorraine.
Space probes / Lorraine Stiegler.
    p. cm. — (Exploring Earth and space)
Includes index.
ISBN: 978-1-4488-8869-6
6-pack ISBN: 978-1-4488-8870-2
ISBN: 978-1-4488-8580-0 (library binding)
1. Space probes—Juvenile literature. 2. Outer space—Exploration—Juvenile literature. I. Title.
TL795.3.S74 2013
629.43'54—dc23

2012014578

Manufactured in the United States of America

CPSIA Compliance Information: Batch #WS12RC: For further information contact Rosen Publishing, New York, New York at 1-800-237-9932.

Word Count: 517

Contents

How Do Space Probes Work?

Space probes are spaceships. **Scientists** use them to gather facts about bodies in space. People don't fly in space probes.

Many space probes study the large bodies in space that move around the sun. These are called planets. Space probes can land on planets or fly by them. Some move in a path called an orbit around the planet.

5

Early Space Probes

Earth is one of the eight planets in our **solar system**. The first American space probe studied Earth. *Explorer 1* went into space on January 31, 1958.

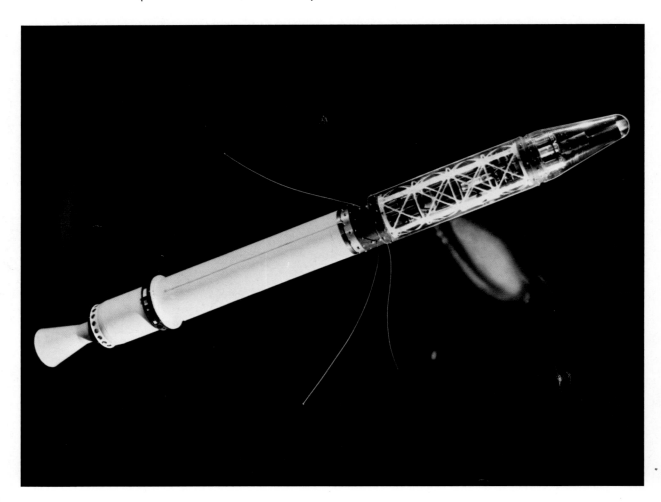

The first space probe to study another planet was
Mariner 2. It flew past Venus on December 14, 1962.
It helped scientists learn that Venus is very hot.

7

In 1965, *Mariner 4* took pictures of Mars.

In 1971, *Mariner 9* began an orbit around Mars.

It was the first space probe to orbit another planet!

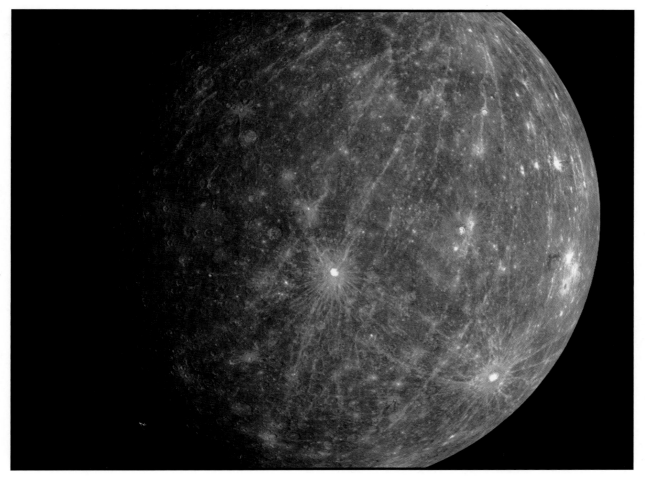

Mariner 10 was the first space probe to visit Mercury. Mercury is the closest planet to the sun. *Mariner 10* flew by Venus and Mercury in 1974 and 1975.

9

The first space probes to land on another planet were
Viking 1 and *Viking 2*. They went into space in 1976
and landed on Mars. Their job was to study the **surface**
of the planet.

10

Exploring the Outer Planets

Some space probes study the outer planets. In 1977, *Voyager 1* went into space. It **explored** Jupiter and Saturn before going to the edge of our solar system.

Pioneer 10 took the first pictures of Jupiter. *Pioneer 11* studied Saturn. This probe flew past Saturn in 1979 and took pictures of the planet and its rings.

The first space probe to explore the planet Uranus was *Voyager 2* in 1986. This probe gathered more facts than scientists had ever known about Uranus. *Voyager 2* also visited Neptune, the last planet in our solar system.

13

In 1997, the *Cassini* space probe began a trip
to Saturn. It was bigger than any probe built before it!
Cassini was built to study Saturn from an orbit
around the planet.

The *Cassini* space probe was built to study Saturn's rings. It was also built to explore Saturn's many moons.

A Look at Mars

Many space probes have been built to study Mars. Scientists want to learn as much as they can about this planet. Space probes help them do that.

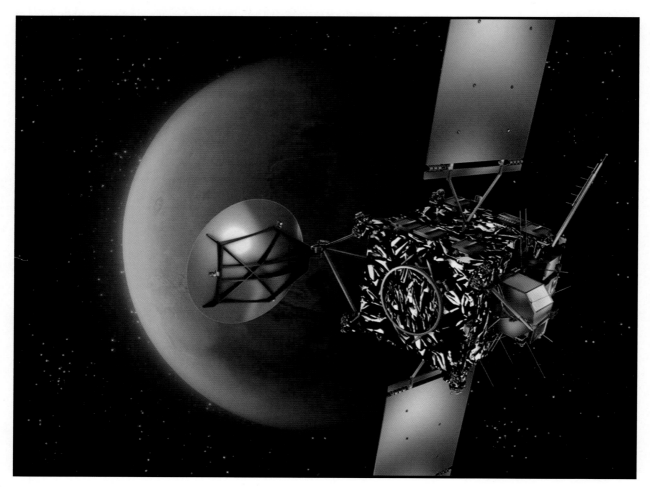

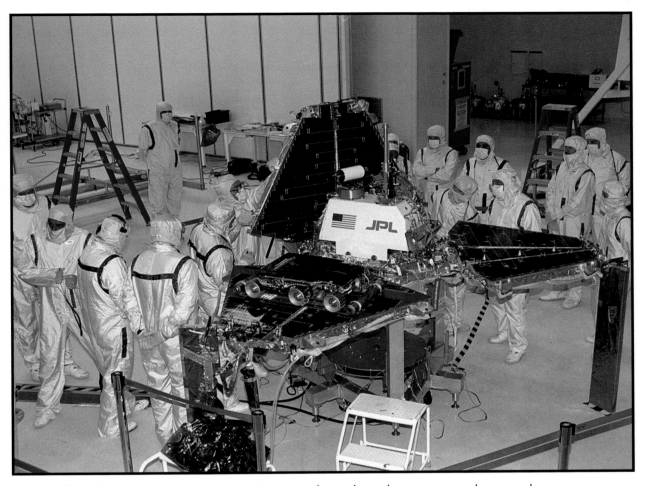

Pathfinder was a space probe built to explore the surface of Mars. It landed on the planet in 1997. Its helped scientists study rocks from Mars.

Pathfinder had a special part called a rover. This is a kind of robot that can move across the surface of a planet. The rover sent lots of pictures back to scientists on Earth.

18

The *Mars Odyssey* space probe began to orbit Mars in 2002. It searched for water on the planet. This probe found lots of ice on Mars.

In 2004, two rovers named *Spirit* and *Opportunity* landed on Mars. They looked for water on the planet's surface and took many pictures to send back to Earth.

20

Still Learning!

Space probes are still being sent out
into the solar system to help us learn more about space.
They are very important tools for space explorers!

Studying Space

1958 — *Explorer 1* studies Earth.

Mariner 2 explores Venus. — **1962**

1965 — *Mariner 4* takes pictures of Mars.

Voyager 1 is sent into space. — **1977**

1986 — *Voyager 2* explores Uranus.

Cassini and *Pathfinder* are sent into space. — **1997**

2004 — *Spirit* and *Opportunity* land on Mars.

Glossary

explore (ihk-SPLOHR) To search something to find out more about it.

scientist (SY-uhn-tihst) A person who studies the way things are and the way things work.

solar system (SOH-luhr SIHS-tuhm) The sun and the objects in space that move around it.

surface (SUHR-fuhs) The top part of something that can be seen.

Index

Due to the changing nature of Internet links, The Rosen Publishing Group, Inc., has developed an online list of websites related to the subject of this book. This site is updated regularly. Please use this link to access the list: **www.powerkidslinks.com/ees/prob**

24